15 MORE AMERICAN ART SONGS

WITH A COMPANION RECORDING OF PIANO ACCOMPANIMENTS

Compiled by Richard Walters

ISBN 978-1-4803-3028-3

G. SCHIRMER, Inc.

DISTRIBUTED BY

HAL•LEONARD®
CORPORATION

7777 W. BLUEMOUND RD. P.O. BOX 13819 MILWAUKEE, WI 53213

www.musicsalesclassical.com
www.halleonard.com

CONTENTS   CD TRACK

Pianist on the recording:
LAURA WARD[1]
RICHARD WALTERS[2]

It's all I have to bring

Emily Dickinson*

Ernst Bacon

*Words printed by special permission.

Hey nonny no!

from *Three Songs: The Words from Old England*

Anonymous (16th century)

Samuel Barber

There are no dynamics in Barber's manuscript; minimal suggestions have been made.

Is't not fine to swim in wine, __ And turn up-on the toe, _____

And sing __ hey non-ny no! When the winds blow and the seas flow?

faster

Hey non-ny no! _____ Hey non-ny no! Hey non-ny no!

slower *a tempo*

[*cresc.*] [***f***]

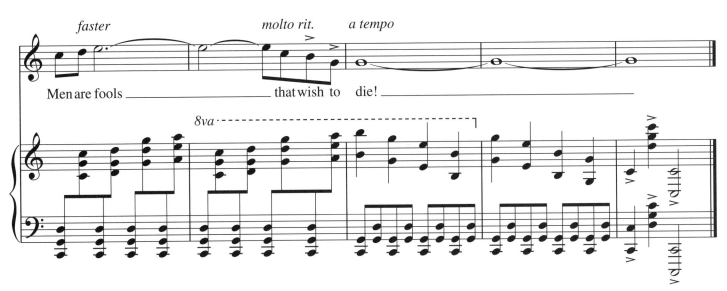

Men are fools _____ that wish to die! _____

faster *molto rit.* *a tempo*

8va -----------------------------

A Slumber Song of the Madonna

Alfred Noyes

Samuel Barber

Here in my arms as I sing thee to sleep! Hush - a - by

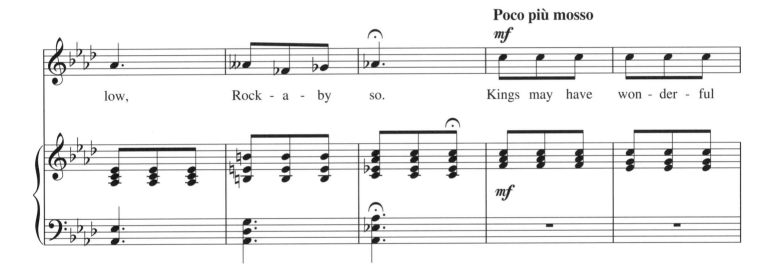

low, Rock - a - by so. Kings may have won - der - ful

Poco più mosso

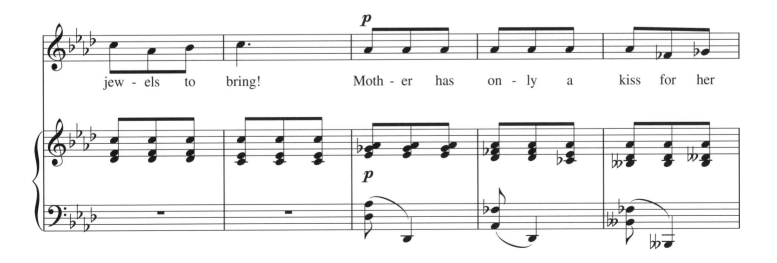

jew - els to bring! Moth - er has on - ly a kiss for her

10

king. Why should my sing - ing So make me to weep?

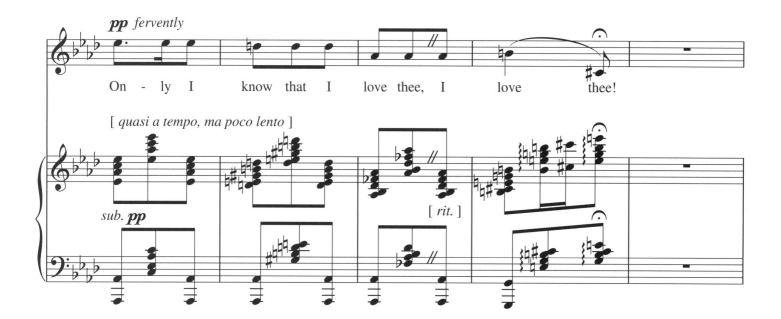

On - ly I know that I love thee, I love thee!

Love thee, my lit - tle one, _____ Sleep!

Mother, I cannot mind my wheel

Walter Savage Landor

Samuel Barber

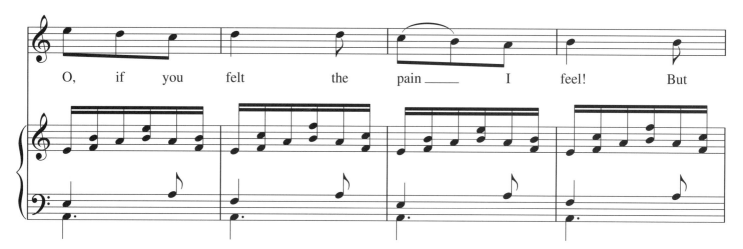

O, if you felt the pain ___ I feel! But

O, ___ who ev - er felt ___ as I? ___

___ No long - er

could I doubt him true— All oth - er

men may use de - ceit;

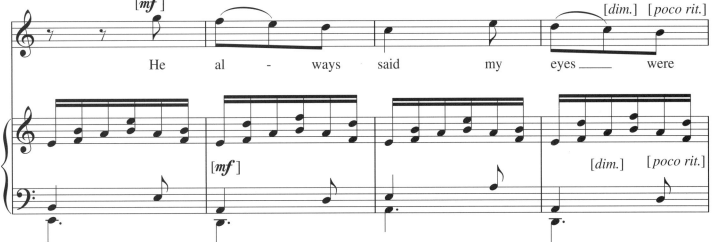

He al - ways said my eyes ____ were

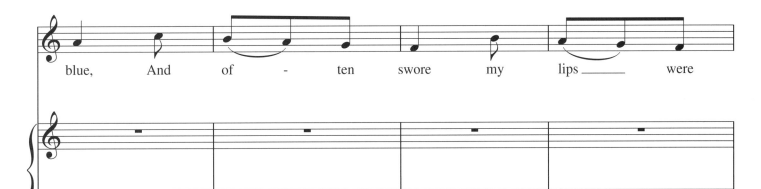

blue, And of - ten swore my lips ____ were

sweet.

The year's at the spring

from *Three Browning Songs,* Op. 44

Robert Browning

Amy Marcy Cheney Beach

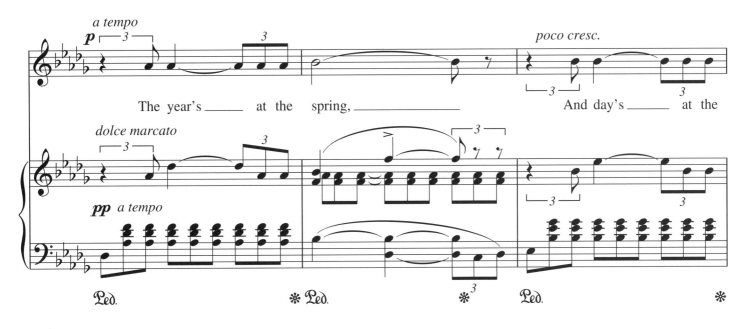

The year's ____ at the spring, ____ And day's ____ at the

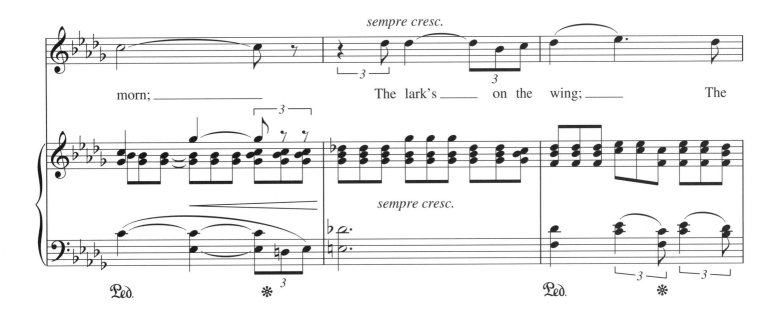

morn; ____ The lark's ____ on the wing; ____ The

snail's ____ on the thorn; ____ God's ____ in His

heaven, _____ God's _____ in His heaven, All's _

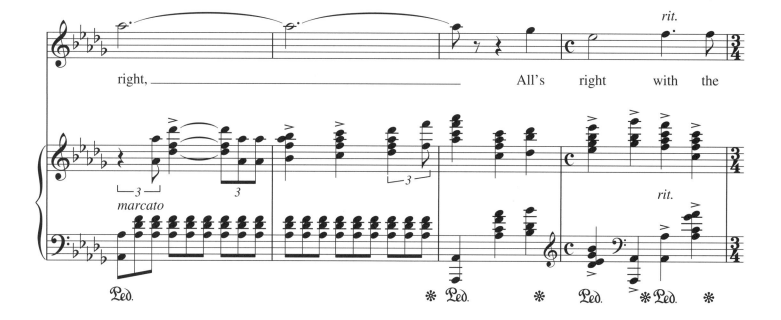

right, _____ All's right with the

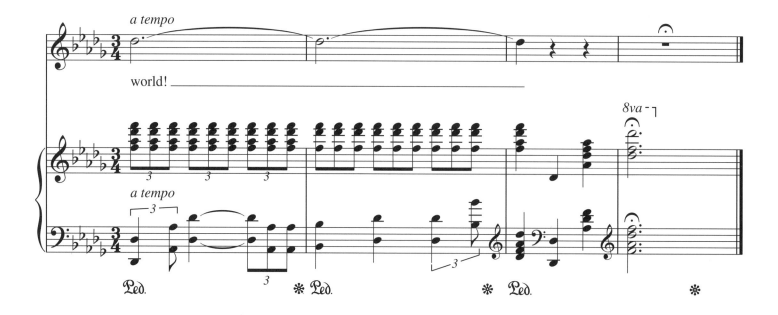

world! _____

Where the Music Comes From

Words and Music by
Lee Hoiby

I want to be where the mu - sic

comes from, Where the clock stops, where it's now. I want to

be with the friends a - round me Who have found me, who show me

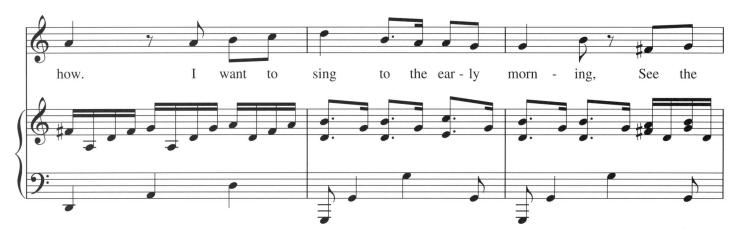

how. I want to sing to the ear-ly morn - ing, See the

sun - light melt the snow; And oh,_____ I want to

grow._____

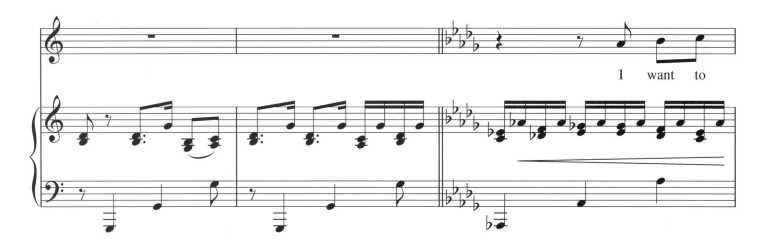

I want to

wake   to the liv-ing spir - it   Here in-side   me where it lies.   I want to

lis - ten till I can hear   it,   Let it guide   me, and   re - al - ize   That I can

go   with the flow un - end - ing,   That is blend - ing,   that is

real;   And   oh, _____   I   want   to

feel.

I want to

walk in the earth - ly gar - den, Far from cit - ies, far from

fear. I want to talk to the grow - ing gar - den, To the

*pronounced *day – vas* (nature spirits)

Sugar in the Cane

Tennessee Williams

Paul Bowles

In absolutely strict tempo ♩ = 66

Voice

Piano

I'm red pep-per in a shak-er, Bread that's wait-in' for the

ba - ker. ___ I'm sweet sug - ar in the cane, ___

Nev - er touched ex - cept by rain. ___

If you touched me God save you, These sum - mer days are hot and

blue. ___

I'm po - ta - toes not yet mashed, I'm a check that ain't been

cashed. _____ I'm a win - dow with a blind, _

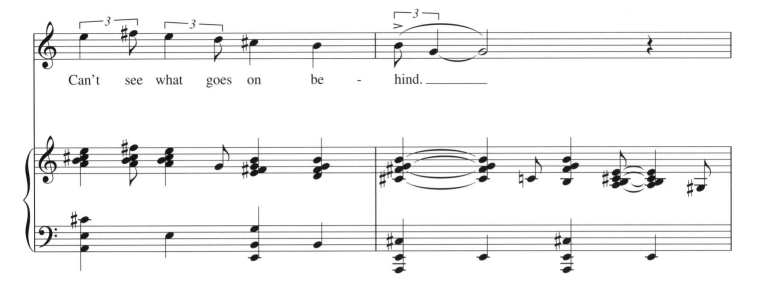

Can't see what goes on be - hind. _____

If you did, God save your soul! These win - ter nights are blue and

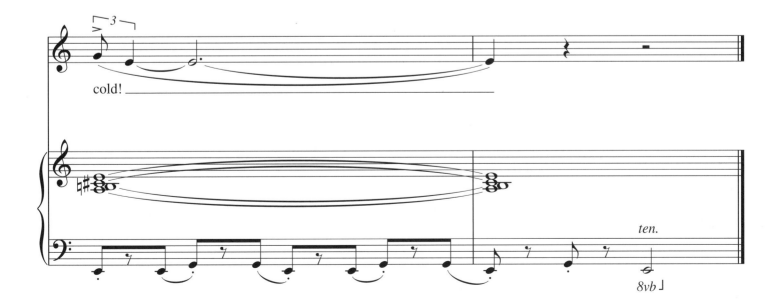

cold! _____

ten.

8vb

February Twilight

Sara Teasdale

John Duke

A sin - gle star _____ looked out From the

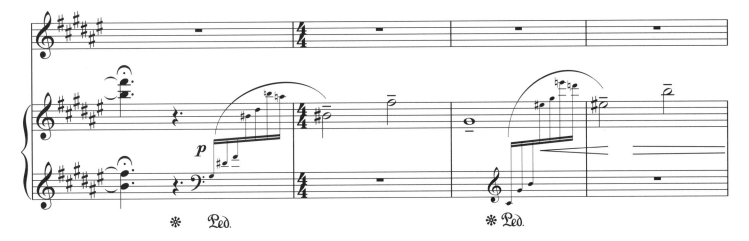

cold eve - ning glow. _____

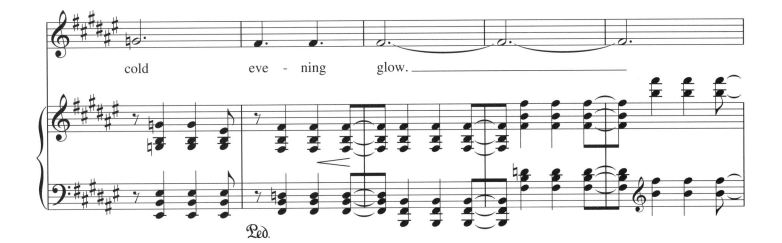

Quasi recitativo

There was no oth - er crea - ture That

Tempo I°

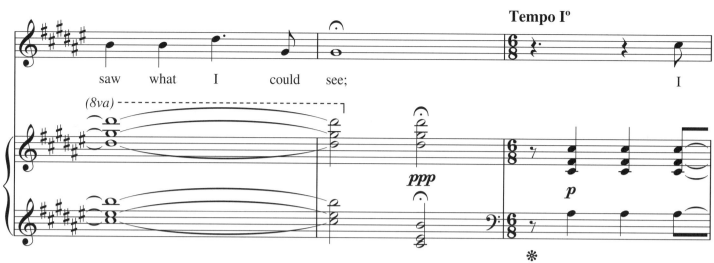

saw what I could see; I

stood and watched the eve - ning

star As long as it watched

me.

To Miriam Witkin

The Green Dog

Words and Music by
Herbert Kingsley

on it. _____ Shoes of leaf - green,

Hose of tea - green, Coat of ap - ple - green, Gloves _ of _ bot - tle - green,

In fact, I nev - er would be seen ex - cept in

green _ If my dog were green.

But, a - las! no mat - ter what you've heard, The facts are con - sis - tent - ly ab -

surd, _____ For my dog is - n't green, _____

And, what sets the mat - ter e - ven more a - gog—

ff

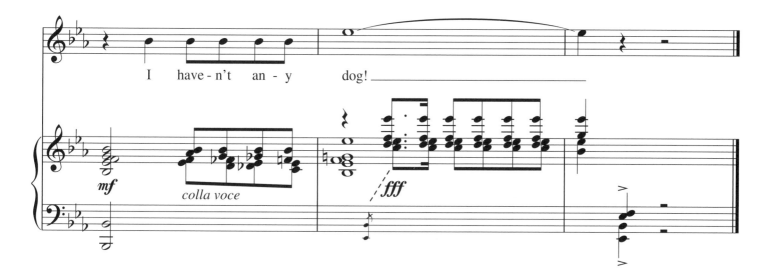

I have - n't an - y dog! _____

mf

colla voce

fff

In the mornin'

Negro spiritual (before 1850) communicated
to Ives in 1929 by Mary Evelyn Stiles

Accompaniment by
Charles Ives

The first chord is played as an introduction on the accompaniment recording.

To Mme. Povla Frijsh

The Pasture

Robert Frost*

Charles Naginski

*From "Collected Poems" by Robert Frost. By permission of Henry Holt and Company, Publishers.

wait   to watch the   wa - ter   clear, _____   I   may):

I   sha'n't be gone   long. —   You   come too.

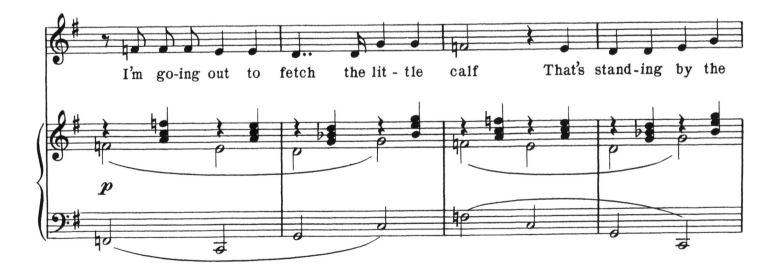

I'm go-ing out   to   fetch   the lit - tle   calf   That's stand-ing by the

moth - er. It's so young, It tot-ters when she

licks it with her tongue.

I sha'n't be gone long.— You come too.

Holiday Song

Genevieve Taggard*

William Schuman
Arranged by the composer

Tempo I moderato ♩ = circa 100

When was it ev - er a waste of time to climb___ hills___ ___ or to sing on our hills the song of a long jol-ly day in the sun?

Tempo I ♩ circa 100 *(no slower)*

All of us, ev - 'ry - one,

ev - 'ry - one, all of us, all of us, ev - 'ry - one, ev - 'ry - one,

fff with energy and precision

stacc. sempre

all of us, ev-'ry-one of us, ev-'ry-one of us, ev-'ry-one of us,

ev - 'ry-one of us, all of us, ev-'ry - one, all of us,

𝅗𝅥 = 𝅗𝅥. **preceding**

fff

fff

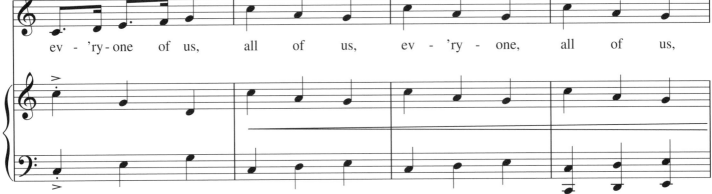

ev - 'ry-one, all of us, ev-'ry-one of us has

𝅗𝅥 = 𝅗𝅥

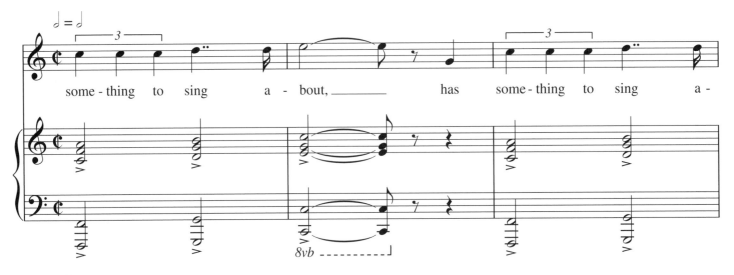

some - thing to sing a - bout, _____ has some - thing to sing a -

8vb _____

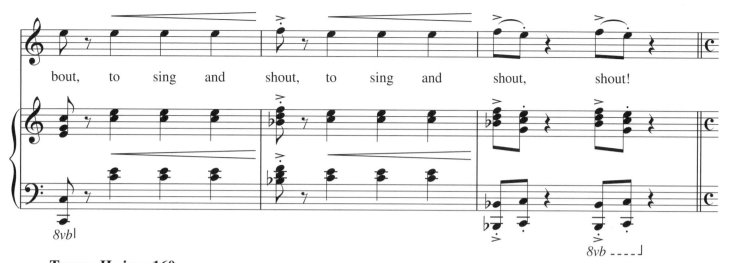

bout,   to sing and shout, to sing and shout, shout!

Tempo II circa 160

Lo!   Dee - de - lee dee, dee - de - lee dee,

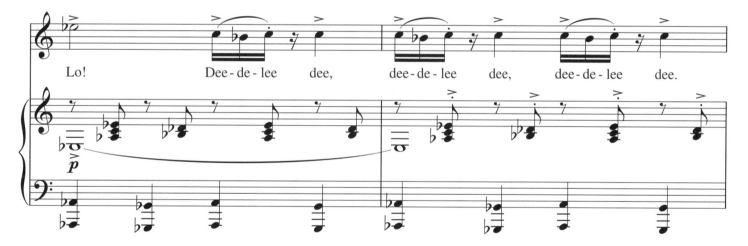

Lo!   Dee - de - lee dee, dee - de - lee dee, dee - de - lee dee.

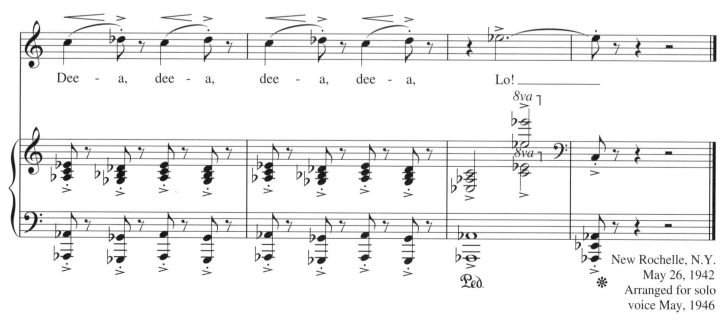

Dee - a, dee - a, dee - a, dee - a, Lo!

New Rochelle, N.Y.
May 26, 1942
Arranged for solo
voice May, 1946

Black is the color of my true love's hair

Text collected and adapted by
John Jacob Niles
Music by John Jacob Niles

love ___ the grass where - on she stands.

I ___ love my_ love and_ well she knows, I

love ___ the grass where-on she goes; If__ she on__ earth no__

more__ I__ see, My life____ will quick-ly leave me.

I__ go to_Troub-le-some* to mourn, to weep, But

sat - is-fied I ne'er can sleep; I'll__ write her a note in__

a few lit-tle lines, I'll suf - fer death ten thou-sand times.

* Troublesome Creek, which empties into the Kentucky River.

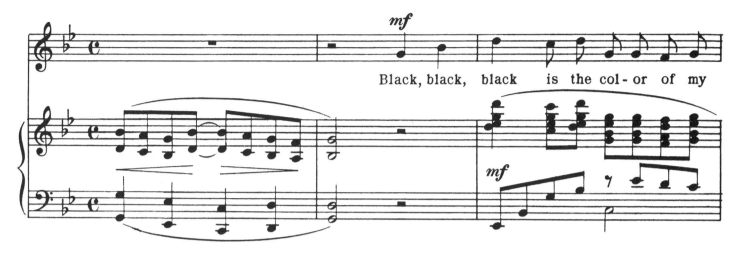

Black, black, black is the col-or of my

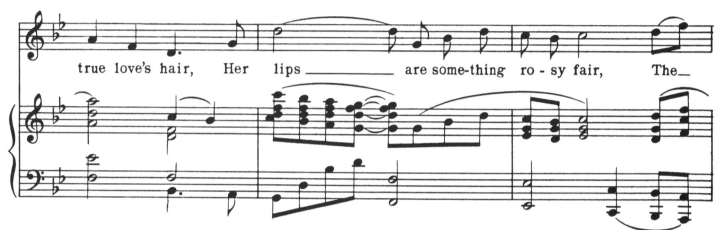

true love's hair, Her lips _____ are some-thing ro - sy fair, The_

pert - est_ face and the dain-ti -est_ hands— I love____ the grass where-

on she stands.

Go 'way from my window

Words and Music by
John Jacob Niles
Arranged by the composer

both- er me no more. I'll
long as song - birds sing. I'll
on ac- count of you. Go
real- ly did love best. Go 'way from my win-dow, Go

'way from my door, Go 'way, 'way, 'way from my bed - side And

both- er me no more, And both- er me no more.

Brother Will, Brother John

Elizabeth Charles Welborn

John Sacco

50

Will, Broth-er John, Broth-er Will, Broth-er John, Broth-er

Will, Broth-er John.

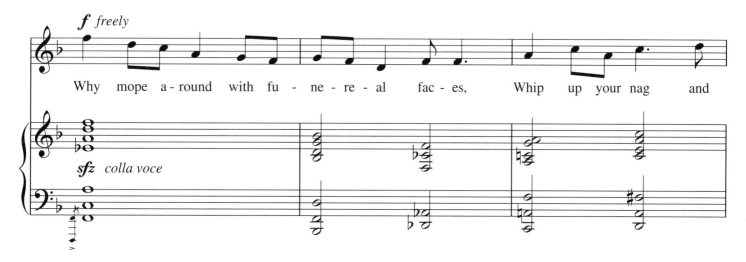

f freely

Why mope a-round with fu-ne-re-al fac-es, Whip up your nag and

sfz colla voce

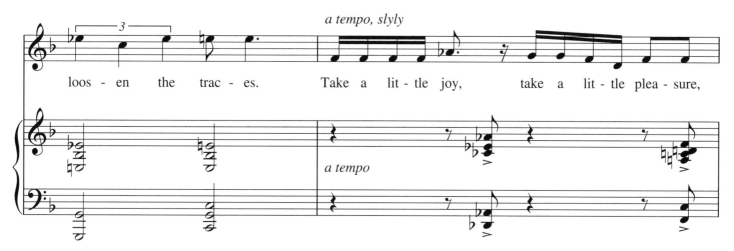

loos-en the trac-es. Take a lit-tle joy, take a lit-tle plea-sure,

a tempo, slyly

a tempo

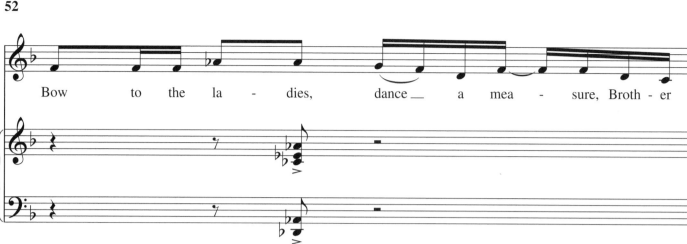

Bow to the la - dies, dance a mea - sure, Broth - er

Will, Broth - er John, Broth - er Will, Broth - er John, Broth - er

Will, Broth-er John.

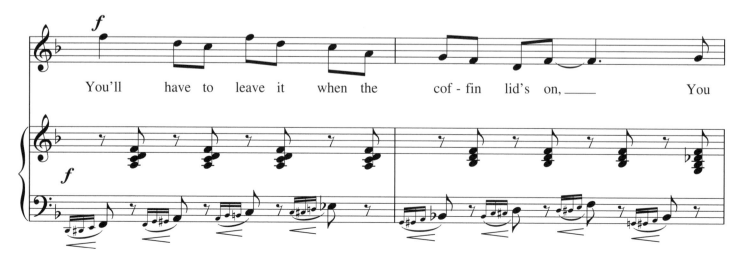

You'll have to leave it when the cof - fin lid's on, You

About the Enhanced CD

In addition to piano accompaniments playable on both your CD player and computer, this enhanced CD also includes tempo and pitch adjustment software for computer use only. This software, known as the Amazing Slow Downer, was originally created for use in pop music to allow singers and players the freedom to independently adjust both tempo and pitch elements. Because we believe there may be valuable educational use for these features in classical and theatre music, we have included this software as a tool for both the teacher and student. For quick and easy installation instructions of this software please see below.

In recording a piano accompaniment we necessarily must choose one tempo. Our choice of tempo, phrasing, ritardandos, and dynamics is carefully considered. But by the nature of recording, it is only one choice. Similar to our choice of tempo, much thought and research has gone into our choice of key for each song.

However, we encourage you to explore your own interpretive ideas, which may differ from our recordings. This new software feature allows you to adjust the tempo up and down without affecting the pitch. Likewise, the Amazing Slow Downer allows you to shift pitch up and down without affecting the tempo. We recommend that these new tempo and pitch adjustment features be used with care and insight. Ideally, you will be using these recorded accompaniments and the Amazing Slow Downer for practice only.

The audio quality may be somewhat compromised when played through the Amazing Slow Downer. This compromise in quality will not be a factor in playing the CD audio track on a normal CD player or through another audio computer program.

INSTALLATION FROM DOWNLOAD:

For Windows (XP, Vista or 7):
1. Download and save the .zip file to your hard drive.
2. Extract the .zip file.
3. Open the "ASD Lite" folder.
4. Double-click "setup.exe" to run the installer and follow the on-screen instructions.

For Macintosh (OSX 10.4 and up):
1. Download and save the .dmg file to your hard drive.
2. Double-click the .dmg file to mount the "ASD Lite" volume.
3. Double-click the "ASD Lite" volume to see its contents.
4. Drag the "ASD Lite" application into the Application folder.

INSTALLATION FROM CD:

For Windows (XP, Vista or 7):
1. Load the CD-ROM into your CD-ROM drive.
2. Open your CD-ROM drive. You should see a folder named "Amazing Slow Downer." If you only see a list of tracks, you are looking at the audio portion of the disk and most likely do not have a multi-session capable CD-ROM.
3. Open the "Amazing Slow Downer" folder.
4. Double-click "setup.exe" to install the software from the CD-ROM to your hard disk. Follow the on-screen instructions to complete installation.
5. Go to "Start," "Programs" and find the "Amazing Slow Downer Lite" application. Note: To guarantee access to the CD-ROM drive, the user should be logged in as the "Administrator."

For Macintosh (OSX 10.4 or higher):
1. Load the CD-ROM into your CD-ROM drive.
2. Double-click on the data portion of the CD-ROM (which will have the Hal Leonard icon in red and be named as the book).
3. Open the "Amazing OS X" folder.
4. Double-click the "ASD Lite" application icon to run the software from the CD-ROM, or copy this file to your hard drive and run it from there.

MINIMUM SOFTWARE REQUIREMENTS:

For Windows (XP, Vista or 7):
Pentium Processor: Windows XP, Vista, or 7; 8 MB Application RAM; 8x Multi-Session CD-ROM drive

For Macintosh (OS X 10.4 or higher):
Power Macintosh or Intel Processor; Mac OS X 10.4 or higher; MB Application RAM; 8x Multi-Session CD-ROM drive